Genetically Speaking

poems on fatherhood

Jim Landwehr

Genetically Speaking

Copyright © 2019 by Jim Landwehr

Published by Local Gems Press

www.localgemspoetrypress.com

This book is dedicated to my wife and kids for giving me the opportunity to be the father I am, and also to the fathers and father figures in my life.
I am grateful for you all.

Acknowledgments

I would like to thank Kathrine, Cristina, Sara, Ed, Peggy, John, Mary Jo, Kathie and all the other poets in my life for inspiring me to do the brave and important work we do. A gracious word of thanks to the citizens and board members for the Village of Wales, Wisconsin for my appointment as Poet Laureate. It has been my privilege to serve you and stretch the love of poetry in the community, even if just a little. I would also like to thank the staff at Local Gems Press for believing in me and publishing my work. And, finally, I feel it is appropriate to thank those fine publications who have published some of these poems prior to this book, including:

"Hold The Line" - published in Bramble Lit Mag
"Ice Charades" – published in Your Daily Poem
"Wrong Place" – published in The Skinny Poetry Journal

Table of Contents

Unanswered

The questions I have are as numerous
as the scars written on my father's
body that night, his last on earth.
Was he a Chevy or a Ford man?
Pepsi or Coke?

Then, the deeper questions.
Democrat, Republican or Independent?
Martin Luther or Malcolm X?

Of course, the obvious hard questions.
What happened that night?
What was said?
Who threw the first punch?

Some days I wonder what life
would have been like with him in it?
And it occurred to me that
I've had a really great life,
and maybe that's better off left alone.

Built For Speed

Parts of fatherhood are made up
of goldfish crackers on the floor
of the vehicle hurtling through
the hard years of car seats,
sippy cups, *are we there yets*,
and unscheduled potty breaks.

And one day I will design a
van that has a stainless steel
playland in the back that
includes a ball pit, jungle gym,
trapeze, big screen television,
sprinkler system and a floor drain.

It will have a soundproof plexiglass
window between driver and children
with a "don't make me come back there"
volume-escalating warning message
and a rewards-based treat
system for good behavior.

There will be educational announcements
along the route explaining points
of interest, major mileposts, random
dad memories, miles to the next
potty break, the score of the Packer
game and estimated minutes to destination.

Ice Charades

On a whim we went skating at
Como Lake one afternoon
I was sixteen, he fifty something.
He had not skated in 35 years
and his skates looked the part
threadbare laces, dull, rusty blades
leather from a Biblical cow.
I had my hockey stick to balance
he kept his hands in his pockets
striding with middle aged savvy
and extra credit for effort.
On the way home he let me
drive his Datsun with a manual tranny.
I whiplashed us to tears at
every stoplight, stalling, starting
shifting, clutching, stalling, repeat.
We were a couple of fuck-ups
muddling our way into fun
that cold Minnesota winter day
just my stepfather and I.

Lifetime Stories

We used to read together
you and I, every night,
a bedtime ritual that we shared.
It was wind-down time for both
so I let you choose the books
two, sometimes three.
You had your favorites
Seuss and his Foot Book
Carle's Hungry Caterpillar.
Sometimes we went
Where The Wild Things Are
Gave A Mouse A Cookie
or laughed at Silverstein's poems
then said Goodnight Moon
and Goodnight Gorilla.
Now you read biographies
and fantasy novels for pleasure
which makes me think those
hours snuggled together on
on your twin bed paid off
in dividends pages long.

Genetically Speaking

Some of her best
and worst
qualities come from him.
Having a plan.
Expecting bad outcomes.
Arriving ridiculously early.
Needing to be right.
Loving her kids.
Worry that stifles experiences.

The difference between
my wife and her father
is a recognition of
and facing up to
his worst and
the humility to
credit him for
the best.

Stranger

I never knew you
but Mom always said
that you loved your kids.
I'm going to have to
take her at her word.

I never knew you
because you bowed
out before the main
event with me.
What would it be?
Doing 100 in your Pontiac?
Hugging me at graduation?
Grandfather to my kids?

You never knew me
but I don't fault you entirely
most of it falls
on the murderous hands
of those that didn't
know you either
your messages to me

7

written in your blood.

Someday we'll get
to know each other again,
and, believe me,
I have much to tell.

Dust

It is Father's Day in the Boundary Waters wilderness of Minnesota. My oldest brother, his son, my niece and nephew and my own two kids are preparing to canoe back to civilization after a three night stay. This trip is missing my younger brother who passed away the previous August after battling cancer. He was the father of two girls, one of whom is here with us trying to work through her grief. In my dead brother's place is my nephew, whose father passed away of a heart attack at a young age. These two fit the tragic mold set by my own father who was murdered when I was only five years old. It seems this day is more about who is not here, than who is. We are together in our aloneness. I give my niece a handful of her father's ashes and she walks to a nearby boulder at the shoreline. After a brief pause, she tosses his ashes to the wind and into the lake where they shimmer on the surface momentarily, then dissipate. The rest of us stand aside respectfully and process this sacred moment between a daughter and the reflection of her father.

114 Reasons I Love Being A Dad

I saved a school assignment of
my daughter's that reads
114 Reasons My Dad is Super

It ranges from the obvious
He reads to me.
He nice.
He takes me to the park.

To the hearfelt
He dances with me
He's a speisal dad
He takes care of me

To the admittedly hilarious
My dad sings in the sower
My dad fixed our toilit.
He reads adult books.

And even downright fabrications
He makes me cookies (Lie! Ask my wife)
He jogs with me (I did?)

Dad feet smell. (Hey!)

These 114 memories of hers are
now memories of mine and serve
as a reminder that the days are
long and the years short.

Never underestimate your
actions as a parent
they are watching.

Steps

The father of another became the father of me
putting he and I in an awkward position.
There were lots of unknowns to address
not the least of which was what to call each other.
Father? Dad? Pops?
Son? Stepson? Mary's kid?
I always assumed it was better to have a dad
than not, and for about four years it was,
but I soon discovered an unintended glitch.
One of the things he brought to the table
was the drinking problem that changed him
from the father of another to the father of me.

Becoming

I was never sure what to expect
when I signed on for
this fatherhood thing.
It seemed like a distant mysterious land
part enchanting
with a princess and a bard
part terrifying
with dragons and fire.
But I knew all along it was an uncharted
journey I'd always wanted to take
in an attempt to correct the mistakes
made by the fathers of my own story.
Then, on a snowy day in November
it happened.
As I watched my daughter enter this world,
my emotions exceeded me.
But it was when I was leaving
the hospital the next day
loading her car seat into our compact
that the burden set upon me as a father
to raise this child righteously
became abundantly clear.

Hurt

You threw your life away
drank it down with no regard
for those under your watch
and while you said your kids
meant more than anything
you were referring to anything
except yourself and your pain.
I am sure you were more
than you ended up – that
you took a wrong turn
and spun out of control
as I nearly did in my
wild youth - only you were
forty two. It still hurts
what you did to us
hurts.

Floor Time

Wrasslin' time
on the floor
was my favorite
on hands and knees
letting the kids come
at me full-bore
as I feigned the pain
groaned and growled
letting them triumph only
to overturn them
a second later
it was a cage match
without a bar in site.
I miss those little bodies
giving their all
doing their best David
against the Goliath
of their father
to bring down the giant
a battle fought in love.

Covered

For all of his faults
he did love me
I wasn't his blood
but he treated me
like I was
he took me places
camping, football games
the beach, fishing.
Apart from his drinking
he was a decent person
it hurts a little to think
what a better person
he could have been
were it not for the
allure of the bottle.
But like I said,
for all of his faults
he did love me
and that love covers
a lot of sins.

Trenches

My kids once relied on me for most everything.
Feeding, diapering, entertainment, bedtime stories
and on and on.
When they got older it became
easier, but there was still reliance.
Rides to practice, help with homework, allowance,
and on and on.
It seems when I turned fifty, things changed.
I rely on them to do things for my aging self,
change that one setting on my phone,
tell me the name of that one movie with that one
guy,
read the tiny print on this or that bottle of whatever,
check my blindspot while I'm driving,
repeat what they just said because I'm half-deaf,
finish my sentence for me when I stammer on a
placename,
drive and get pizza take out for dinner,
and on and on.
Back then, I was in the trenches of toddlerhood
and now they are entrenched in my middle age.
It only seems fair.

Cover Two

My mother was the hero
my dad was supposed to be
she filled the role of two
picked up the slack
powered through each day
showing us all that
sometimes it takes a strong
mother to fill the gap
left by a displaced father.
She did the best she could
getting up every morning
and living out her life
in sacrifice for those of us
he left thrashing in his wake.

Career Day

When asked what our parents did
for a living, my young son told his
teacher I was an astronaut for NASA.

She asked him where I kept my
spacesuit and he said in the closet
but that I didn't like to talk about it.

While I've never been to outer space
I have to give him credit
he has his father's imagination.

Defining Words

Like nearly every dad alive
he had his goofy sayings

Can of Corn
meant no problem, piece of cake

Not to worry
from his Irish heritage

'Tis a fine, fine fire
drinking cocktails while camping

absolvo te in nomine domini
a reflection of his Catholic upbringing

Name that tune
a spontaneous guessing game

Salt of the earth
what he called people close to his heart

About a three beer run

an estimate of his vacation drives.

High cheekbones and no split ends
an awkward introduction of his daughters

Where there is one, there are dozens more
some uttered to get a laugh, others drunken phrases

But all of them conjure memories from the vapor
of who our stepfather once was

Paddling With Purpose

It is a breezy day in our canoe on a lake in the Boundary Waters Canoe Area of Minnesota. My daughter and I battle the gusty winds, ultimately seeking shelter of a large island. She is disappointed in the fishing thus far, though we've only been camping a single night. Her impatience with the fish is part of what I love about her. After we find a calm spot, she casts and lands a nice walleye. Then another. Then I get one. She another. Her mood changes from somber and scowling to expectant and radiant. And as I sit in the canoe I realize this moment will live forever within both of us. It is a moment of connection between father and daughter in the middle of both nowhere and everywhere. She's wearing a dirty shirt and hiding a bad case of camping hair underneath a backwards Cornhuskers hat. Despite all of that, at this moment she is the most beautiful girl in my world.

Mom

She is asleep
her infant son, Paul
in the bassinet
beside her bed
her other five kids
in their rooms
slumbering on this warm
June night.

None of them
knows the fate
that they will
wake to with
the morning's
first rays.

As the saying goes,
there IS a fate
worse than death.
It is life after *this* death.
Death of a husband.
Death of a father.

Murder of an innocent.

The telephone rings.

Food For Thoughts

There was that time you were
craving gut bombs so you took us
to White Castle and bought 28 bombs,
six boxes of nails and a few gobblers.
The menu read differently.
On occasion when your sweet
tooth kicked in after dinner and
you'd say we should go to 71 Flavors
which was your play on Baskin Robbins.
I always had Pineapple Ice.
And you had a thing for the cheapest
beer you could find at the liquor store
Hauenstein and Blatz which are
better described as crappy and crappier.
Your cigarettes of choice were
True because they were low tar
a slower, less pleasurable method
of corporate assisted suicide.
Every once in a while you had
corned beef hash with a soft boiled
egg on it for breakfast.
While I could fathom all of

the other culinary and eccentricities
of vice, this one was incomprehensible.
But when combined with all the rest
it sort of summed up how you lived
your life, outside the lines
your way.

Little Girl

She is with her boyfriend
and I cannot help but notice
how they touch each other.
She leans into him
they walk holding hands
he rubs her back as they sit.
It is all good human contact
but she was once mine
her body much smaller.
She used to lean into me
we held hands as we walked
just like they do now.
This turning of the tables
is part of life's natural course
but that doesn't mean I have
to like it or embrace it
though it does mean that
she has taken the love I have
shown and made it her own
keeping it for her lifetime.

Missed

He wasn't there
for my sixth birthday
eighth grade football games
my high school graduation
or college
not when I moved away
not my wedding
not the birth of my daughter
or son
never gave job advice
or girlfriend advice
never helped fix my car
or took me to a ball game.
Instead
my sister taught me to ride a bike
my brother how to work a drill
my mother how to treat others
and others filled in the gaps
but I had to figure out the rest
on my own.
These are the things
taken from me

on that night
in June
of '67.

You and I

I hope I was there when you
needed me to show you my pride.
I wonder if I did all I could
to inspire you to be your best?
I pray you will find someone
who you can share your life with.
You prove to me every day
that I never gave you enough credit.
You texted me when I was down
and helped me through a tough week.
You will always be my special boy
even as we stand eye to eye.
I love you, son.

Head Of The House?

On the phone with tech support,
I suddenly become frantic
when I cannot find my phone
the one I am speaking into

When discussing a particular movie
at dinner with my kids, I reference
that gruesome scene on Omaha Beach
in the movie Saving Private Benjamin

Just a day after I buy a new $800 phone,
I worry, fret and self-loathe about the scratch
I see on the screen, that I later find out
is on the out-of-the-box filmy screen protector

I bake a cake with my kids
as a surprise for my wife
and in the frosted words, Happy Birthday
I use gel food coloring thinking it's frosting

I'm not sure when it happened
when I was no longer the smartest

in my household but
I think it started at fatherhood

Recall

There was that one time
when you let me steer the car
it was scary fun

I remember you
took me out alone one time
two boys all grown up

That one time us kids
snuck up behind your big chair
and messed up your hair

You were on the phone
calling a cab for your friend
he was pretty drunk

This is the extent
the sum total of all my
memories of you

The Difference

I try and imagine what it
would be like if I had not
raised my two children.
I suppose it would be
like having a hot fudge
sundae without the fudge
or a maraschino cherry.
Like nonalcoholic beer
or a cold decaf coffee.
Being a parent has been
a test of selflessness
dedication, effort and a
new found ability to reach
a Lego lost under a chair.
But it has given my days
depth, contour and
a holy, almighty richness
it has dressed them in
a comfortable sweater
and kissed them on
the nave of their neck.

Missteps

I wish

I could have taken the happiness
you wore when you were drinking
and woven it into a vest of contentment
to keep the sadness out of your heart

those you hurt with your drunken words
had a chance to hear your sorrys
and use them like a bandage of redemption
to heal the wounds you never intended

that I could take our fondest memories
play them back one frame at a time
like a movie of dad's epic moments
to remind us of what lay beneath

that I had a chance to thank you
for the good you did despite the rest
these silver linings to your clouded past
diamonds in the rough of your life

Surrogate

I learned how to fish from my older brother.
He taught me how to shoot a shotgun,
paddle a canoe, tie a Windsor knot
stressed the importance of a good sleeping bag
helped me practice drive on my learner's permit
and showed me basic lawnmower maintenance.
What he didn't give me was
the love and assurance that I was
more important to him
than most everything
or that he would step in front
of a train to save my life.
And while his presence in my life
served as a decent stopgap
a sort of surrogate dad,
there are innate emotions,
core responses and fundamental truths
that can only be passed on by a father.
Things like, how to treat a woman
the confidence-inducing "Attaboy"
a rib-crushing man hug
but most of all the words
I love you, son.

Wrong Place (A skinny poem)

Life without him
father
children
absent
foundation
father
drinking
racial
murder
father
Him without life

Second Career

I worried during my wife's pregnancies
that the little bodies within were healthy.

When they were born I worried that
they would die in their sleep of SIDS.

As they grew up in elementary school
the worry was about friends and fitting in.

High school brought the worrisome
subjects of sex, drugs and alcohol.

College meant worrying over tuition,
jobs, grades and a good experience.

I thought when they graduated
that the worry would go away.

I'm now fully convinced that
as a parent, worry is a life skill.

Holy Moments

There are pivotal moments in the life of a dad
moments that make one pause or gasp at the sanctity.
That infant nap on your chest, those first footsteps,
the separation anxiety of kindergarten.
Each one brings parent and child closer to
the fullest expression of themselves.
That squeaky middle school violin recital,
junior prom in a dress that shows the future,
a personal best at the last swim meet.
These are the times that set our place
in the collapsing universe of one another
and before he can say he is proud of them,
they fly and he is left with loving emptiness.

Levelling Up

Though I've done my best
faking my way through this
fatherhood gig like I almost
knew what I was doing,
there are others I know
who have done far more,
far better than myself.
Like my selfless friends
who adopted three
one more than we dared raise.
Or the ones that fostered
six only to adopt them later.
Theirs is a fearless love.
And there are those who know
themselves well enough to
say no to parenthood altogether.
That is fearless recognition
a choice for both parent and child.

Cheated

I am in a boat
in northern Wisconsin
with my son and
daughter.
We are fishing
and while the bite
is light, I relish
the moment
knowing that it
isn't
really
about
the
fish.
As I bait hooks
and uncross lines
it occurs to me
that as a kid I was
cheated in the
whole deal.
And I want to
stop my kids

for just a moment
and say,
"Do you know
how lucky you are?"

What It Takes

to be a father? I can only speak from my own experience. It takes being there when your wife goes fetal in the shower from exhaustion. It takes wrestling on the floor with your four and one year old. And lots of sippy cups, binkies, sinus-burning diapers and a metric ton of patience - administered daily. Of course, discipline when needed and stories at bedtime, both real and made up from your own imagination. It takes late night feedings when they're babies and late night worries when they're off at prom. Oh, and dancing to the stereo when they're little. Dance with them a lot. But most of all it takes your presence clothed in the finely tailored suit of a father's love. A presence that *never* leaves. Ever.

Unconventional Wisdom

At the age of twenty my college-aged son
stands a few inches shorter than me
lean and muscular, growing the scruffy
beard I was never brave enough to grow.
I cannot help but to worship all that
he's become and the young life
that lays stretched out before him.

Of course as a man much older
and as his father, I have much advice.
Finish college. Have fun along the way
but remember why you are there and finish
because no one hires half a degree.

Sort out those one or two lifetime friends
the ones who know your faults,
quirks, idiosyncracies and favorite bands.
You may lose touch when you raise families
but they will come back to you in your fifties
and pick up in the middle of the laugh you
left with.

I daresay have some chemical fun, pot and booze,
laugh until it hurts, talk smart, solve world
problems
but then lose the pipe and temper the thirst
because life is too short to spend in a haze
with a bad short term memory or a police record.

If the opportunity arises to go to California
or Maine or Canada, make it happen
even if it means sleeping on a crappy couch
or eating frozen burritos and granola for a week
because next to formal education, travel
will teach you that the world you live in
is a lot bigger and your problems much smaller.

Find God in something you do, somewhere you go,
a hobby, craft or someone that reminds you
of Him.
Because I guarantee you at some point in life
you will need something more than a human
can give
to make sense of a senseless tragedy or loss
and, besides, His unconditional love is a bet
worth hedging.

Work hard for forty years, show up early, stay late

never stop learning, listen to your coworkers
learn from their mistakes and run from gossip,
congratulate the one that gets a promotion in front
of you, as it speaks volumes about who you are.

Be a loving husband or father, godfather
or uncle, brother or cousin, or just a good man.
Write or say those things that men struggle
to say for fear of being labeled sensitive
because your success and fame will fade
from peoples' minds far before your words.

About the Author

Jim has four poetry collections, *Reciting from Memory*, *Written Life, On a Road* and *Thoughts From A Line At The DMV*. Jim also has two nonfiction books, *Dirty Shirt: A Boundary Waters Memoir* and *The Portland House: A '70s Memoir*. His poetry has been featured in *Rosebud, Cirrus Poetry Review, Blue Heron Review* and many others. His nonfiction stories have been published in *Main Street Rag*, *Prairie Rose Publications*, *Story News, The Sun,* and others. He lives in Waukesha, Wisconsin with his wife, Donna. He enjoys fishing, kayaking, biking and camping. Jim is the 2018-2019 poet laureate for the Village of Wales, Wisconsin. For more on his work, visit: http://jimlandwehr.com

Photo credit: Roost Photography.

Local Gems Poetry Press is a small Long Island based poetry press dedicated to spreading poetry through performance and the written word. Local Gems believes that poetry is the voice of the people, and as the sister organization of the Bards Initiative, believes that poetry can be used to make a difference.

Local Gems has published over 200 titles.

www.localgemspoetrypress.com

Made in the USA
Monee, IL
01 June 2023

35060537R00036